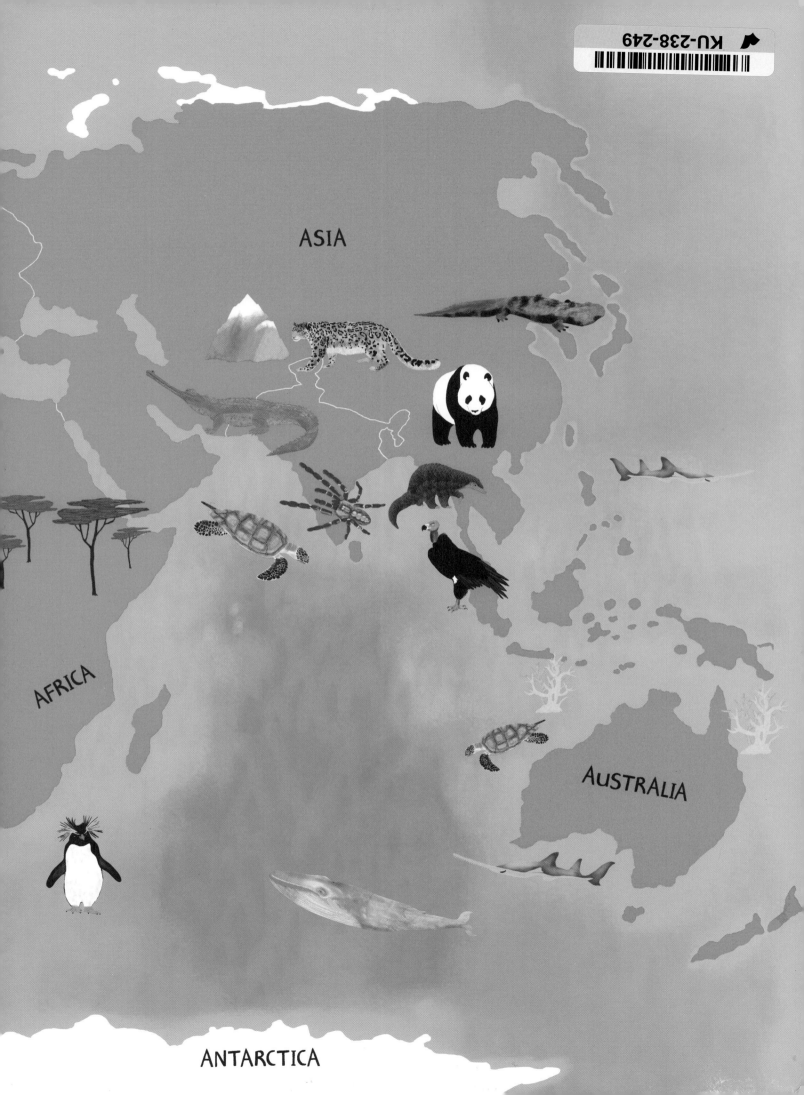

ASIA

AFRICA

AUSTRALIA

ANTARCTICA

For my friend Jeff, who gave me my first job
campaigning for endangered species
at Greenpeace many years ago – CB

For Will, Ella, Mia and Frank the dog.
It's wonderful sharing this incredible planet with you – AW

ACKNOWLEDGEMENTS
The author, illustrator and publishers would like to thank
the following for their help and advice:

Patrick Campbell, Senior curator, Reptiles,
Natural History Museum, London, UK

Jeff Canin, former Greenpeace International sea turtle campaigner

Dr Dean Grubbs, Associate Director of Research,
Florida State University Coastal and Marine Laboratory, USA

Craig Hilton-Taylor, Head Red List Unit, Global Species Programme,
IUCN (International Union for Conservation of Nature)

Professor Jeffrey Lang, Biology, University of North Dakota, USA

Lorna Lawson, Head of Programmes Content, WWF-UK

Dr Nisha Owen, EDGE of Existence Programme Manager,
Zoological Society of London, UK

Dr Jeff Streicher, Curator, Amphibians,
Natural History Museum, London, UK

Text copyright © Catherine Barr 2018

Illustrations copyright © Anne Wilson 2018
First published in Great Britain in 2018 by
Otter-Barry Books, Little Orchard, Burley Gate, Herefordshire, HR1 3QS
www.otterbarrybooks.com

This paperback edition first published in Great Britain in 2020

ISBN 978-1-91307-492-0

Illustrated with mixed media and digital art

Printed in China

9 8 7 6 5 4 3 2 1

Red Alert!

15 endangered animals fighting to survive

Written by
Catherine Barr

Illustrated by
Anne Wilson

Otter-Barry BOOKS

"The International Union for
Conservation of Nature (IUCN) Red List
tells us where we urgently need to
do something to prevent
the despoliation of this world.
It is a great agenda for the work
of conservationists."

Sir David Attenborough

Around the world scientists are collecting stories, facts and figures that help us understand and care for life on Earth. Some of these scientists are working together to create a gigantic **Red List** of animals, plants and fungi.

It is red because many of the 80,000 species investigated so far are in danger of disappearing. The information gathered for this **Red List** is used to help save endangered species.

So let's get started...
Pick a place
Choose a favourite creature
Discover its story
Help to save it

Pick a Place

deserts

forests

mountains

grasslands

rivers

oceans

Pick your favourite place.
Then turn the page to choose a
rare creature that lives there.

Choose a Creature

mountains

grasslands

deserts

page 28

page 30

page 32

oceans

page 36

forests

page 34

page 40

rivers

page 24

page
26

page
22

page
14

page
18

page
12

page
38

Choose a creature that lives in your favourite place. Then go to its page to discover its story.

page
20

page
16

11

Meet the
Blue Whale
Mammal
Balaenoptera musculus

A shadowy story

The Blue Whale is the biggest animal that has ever lived on Earth. But from their boat, the whale watchers catch only her blurred shadow as she disappears. She is singing mysterious songs that echo, unheard by humans, for miles around her vast watery home.

FACTS: * The Blue Whale swims in oceans all round the world, except the Arctic *

* Its song is louder than a jet plane *

* It has the biggest babies on Earth and its arteries are so big that a toddler could crawl along them *

* Killing Blue Whales was banned by the International Whaling Commission in 1966 *

Whales were once at home on land. But millions and millions of years ago, their legs became fins and they returned to the sea where all life began. But this streamlined ocean giant has been hunted to the edge of extinction. So the whale-watching tourists are lucky to spot one at all.

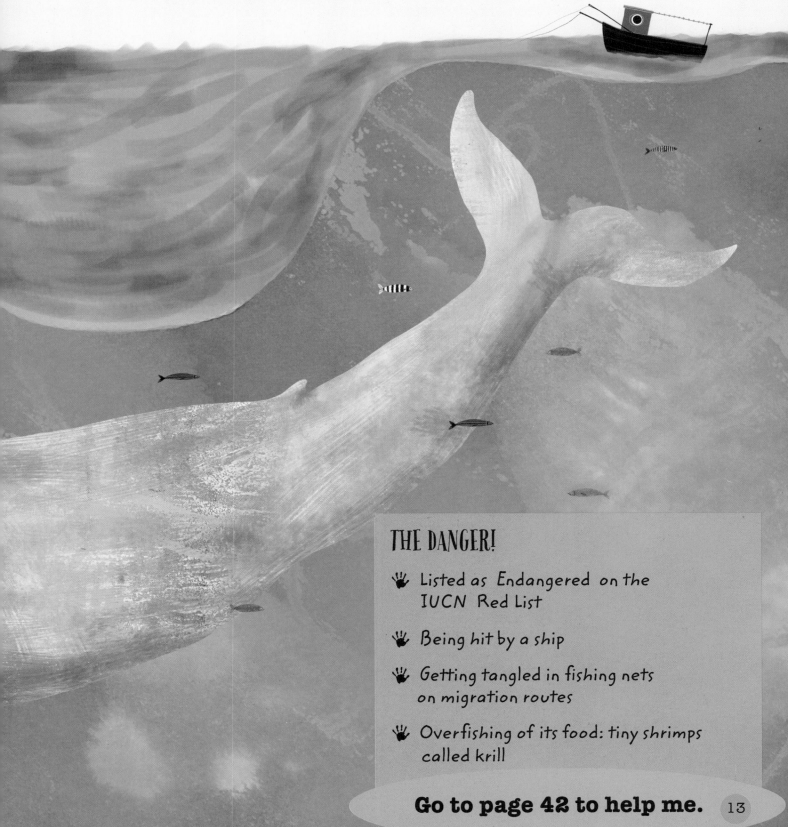

THE DANGER!

- ✋ Listed as Endangered on the IUCN Red List
- ✋ Being hit by a ship
- ✋ Getting tangled in fishing nets on migration routes
- ✋ Overfishing of its food: tiny shrimps called krill

Go to page 42 to help me.

Meet the
Sunda Pangolin
Mammal
Manis javanica

A shy story

The most hunted animal in the world rolls up into a ball, covering its head with its front legs. It is scared. But this one is lucky, rescued by a wildlife ranger from smugglers who are after its meat and scales. Its scales are dried and used in traditional Chinese medicines.

FACTS: * The Sunda Pangolin lives in grasslands and forests across Southeast Asia *

* Its tongue can be longer than its body *

* In Malay its name means 'something that rolls up' *

* It is one of the few mammals completely covered in scales *

The Sunda Pangolin is shy and secretive. It wanders around at night, sniffing out termites and ants to lap up with a long sticky tongue. Its scales protect it from predators like tigers. But human hunters just pick it up when it rolls into a ball. This ranger will tell children the pangolin's story. But away from its natural home, it will be a challenge to help the pangolin survive.

THE DANGER!

- 🖐 Listed as Critically Endangered on the IUCN Red List
- 🖐 Hunted for its meat and scales
- 🖐 Limited conservation funding because it is not a well-known animal
- 🖐 Its forest habitat is threatened by human activities

Go to page 42 to help me.

Meet the
Panamanian Golden Frog

Amphibian

Atelopus zeteki

An unlucky story

Leaping across rocks beneath rushing water, a slippery yellow frog escapes a zookeeper's grasp. To avoid the poisons that protect it from predators, the zookeeper is wearing gloves. He is catching the frog to save it from a mysterious disease sweeping through its forest home and is taking it to a 'frog hotel' where it can breed safely.

FACTS: * The signals it uses are highly unusual in amphibians *

* Its skin is poisonous to humans and other predators *

The Panamanian Golden Frog is famous for its wave. Living close to waterfalls, it uses sign language to attract mates and frighten predators. It is known in Panama as a symbol of good luck. But as the mysterious fungal disease advances, its luck is running out.

* The habitat of the Panamanian Golden Frog is the mountainous cloud forests of Panama, Central America *

THE DANGER!

- 🖐 Listed as Critically Endangered on the IUCN Red List

- 🖐 Threatened by a fatal fungal skin disease

- 🖐 Destruction of its forest habitat to build towns and create farmland

- 🖐 Over-collection for the pet trade

- 🖐 Pollution of its freshwater habitat

Go to page 42 to help me.

Northern Rockhopper Penguin

Bird

Eudyptes moseleyi

A sketchy story

A bird with extraordinary eyebrows is hopping from rock to rock. Perched nearby, a wildlife artist is drawing the Northern Rockhopper Penguin. This one looks cross and she *is* – another bigger bird is trying to steal her eggs.

FACTS * The Northern Rockhopper Penguin is found in the South Atlantic Ocean and Indian Ocean * It nests on rocky and grassy shorelines * Unlike other penguins, it jumps rather than waddles *

THE DANGER!

🖐 Listed as Endangered on the IUCN Red List

🖐 Overfishing of its food: squid and krill

🖐 Getting caught in fishing gear

🖐 Illegal collection of its eggs

Go to page 42 to help me.

Hopping about over rocks in huge colonies, this penguin returns to nest with the same partner each year. Although familiar because its cousin, the Southern Rockhopper Penguin, is a character in the film *Happy Feet*, the wild population of this quirky bird has crashed over the last 30 years. The wildlife artist is trying to capture the personality of this tough little bird.

* It can dive up to 100 metres for fish, crustaceans, squid and krill *

A nosy story

Unable to lift its belly off the sand like other crocodiles,
the enormous Long-nosed Crocodile shuffles up the river
bank. He has many razor-sharp teeth and a lump on
the end of his nose. Across the river, a camera clicks
and this strange-looking reptile is caught on film.

FACTS * The Long-nosed Crocodile lives in large rivers in India and Nepal *

* The male crocodile grows up to six metres long *

* One big male babysits hundreds of babies
in a crocodile nursery *

* The lump on the male's nose is called a *ghara*, the Hindi word for a bowl *

20

In fast-flowing water, these crocodiles (also known as Gharials), use their slender noses to sneak up on fish. Only males have noses with lumps, which they use to make a noise that the females like. The film-maker focuses on the bobbly nose. He wants local children to see the rare river creature that lives so close to their school.

THE DANGER!

- ✋ Listed as Critically Endangered on the IUCN Red List

- ✋ Getting tangled in fishing nets

- ✋ Too little water in its river habitat before the rains

- ✋ Pollution and damming of its river habitats

Go to page 42 to help me.

An ugly story

Vultures are circling above a pile of dead animals while a man watches from his empty truck. He has dumped fresh waste meat for these huge birds. Red-headed Vultures strip the rotting meat from dead animals, leaving a clean pile of bones. This stops diseases spreading.

Where wild food is scarce, Red-headed Vultures prey on dead livestock. But some medicines given to cattle make their meat poisonous to vultures. So these giant birds are dying as they feed more on domestic animals. Staring at the healthy 'vulture restaurant' he has created, the truck driver is glad to help these important birds.

THE DANGER!

 Listed as Critically Endangered on the IUCN Red List

Medicine used to treat livestock in some countries is poisonous to vultures

Poisons used to catch fish and birds at water holes are also killing the vultures

Tall trees that vultures nest in are being cut down for firewood

FACTS: * The Red-headed Vulture lives in wooded hills

* It does amazing aerial cartwheels in courtship dances *

Go to page 42 to help me.

Meet the
Red-headed Vulture
Bird
Sarcogyps calvus

and dry forests across India and Southeast Asia *

* It helps to get rid of dead animals that could spread disease * It only lays one egg each year *

Meet the
Chinese Giant Salamander
Amphibian
Andrias davidianus

A slippery story

The ancestors of this huge slimy creature once swam around the feet of dinosaurs. This one lies still in a cool mountain lake. It's dusk and the largest amphibian in the world is hiding. But before the Chinese Giant Salamander can ambush its prey, it is surprised by a scientist with a notepad.

FACTS * The Chinese Giant Salamander lives in high, rocky mountain streams and some freshwater lakes in China *

* It breathes through its skin *

THE DANGER!

🖐 Listed as Critically Endangered on the IUCN Red List

🖐 Hunted for its meat, considered a delicacy in Asia

🖐 Its habitat is threatened as trees are cut down and soil silts up the rivers

🖐 Pollution of rivers by chemicals from farming

Go to page 42 to help me.

The scientists are careful of the sticky goo that seeps through the salamander's wrinkled skin when it is scared. This keeps it safe from non-human predators. But it is hunted for meat and thousands are farmed for expensive meals. Once measured, this wild one slips back to safety, to surprise crabs, fish and frogs for its supper.

* In Chinese it is called the Infant Fish, as the whining, crying noises it makes sound like a child *

* It is the largest of all living amphibians, growing up to 1.8 metres long *

A stealthy story

Dawn breaks as the Snow Leopard's soft, grey eyes scan the snow. She flicks her thick tail and, stiff with cold, a cameraman stares down his lens at one of the world's rarest big cats. The leopard pads softly into focus.

Unable to roar, this mountain cat lives silently and alone. To catch her prey she must spring into action — leaping across ledges to bring down wild sheep and goats. But the Snow Leopard is very difficult to find, so the cameraman is proud to have caught this secretive snow cat on film at last.

FACTS: * The Snow Leopard lives in the steep, rocky mountains of Central Asia, spanning 12 countries *

* This 'ghost of the mountain' can jump like an acrobat but is shy and difficult to spot *

* It wraps its long, thick tale around itself like a scarf *

* It can't roar but it can hiss, purr and make a puffing chuff noise *

THE DANGER!

🖐 Downlisted from Endangered to Vulnerable on the IUCN Red List due to new population estimates, but more action is still needed

🖐 Illegally hunted for its fluffy fur coat

🖐 Disappearance of its habitat and prey as domestic animals graze bigger areas

🖐 Conflict with people as hungry Snow Leopards steal livestock

Go to page 42 to help me.

27

A slinky story

Slithering from its dusty burrow at sunset,
this soft grey snake has just woken up.
It stretches sleepily across the path.
As a girl wanders past, she almost steps on
its camouflaged body. If the snake had been
able to rattle, the girl would have jumped.

The Santa Catalina Rattlesnake is the only
rattlesnake in the world without a rattle.
Like others, it sheds its skin. But instead of
leaving a hollow rattle at the end of its tail,
its skin just falls off. Without big predators
on the island, there may be no need for the
snake to rattle. The young tourist wanders on,
unaware of her close encounter with this quiet,
dangerous little snake.

It is a stealthy hunter, good at slinking up trees

28

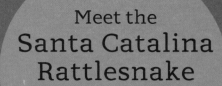

Meet the
Santa Catalina Rattlesnake
Reptile
Crotalus catalinensis

FACTS *The Santa Catalina Rattlesnake lives only on Isla Santa Catalina in the Gulf of California, Mexico *

* It has a heat-sensing 'pit' between its eyes, which helps it find warm-blooded prey *

THE DANGER!

- Listed as Critically Endangered on the IUCN Red List

- Hunted and eaten by domesticated cats that have gone wild

- Caught illegally for the pet trade

- Lack of interest in snakes means that there is often no conservation plan to save them

Go to page 42 to help me.

29

Meet the Hawksbill Sea Turtle

Reptile

Eretmochelys imbricata

An ancient story

Leaving a trail like tyre tracks, the Hawksbill Sea Turtle crawls up the beach to nest, after her exhausting journey. She has crossed the oceans and is here at last to lay her eggs. They fall like soft ping-pong balls into a hole in the sand, as a scientist counts.

FACTS: * The Hawksbill Sea Turtle is mostly found

THE DANGER!

- ✋ Listed as Critically Endangered on the IUCN Red List

- ✋ Hunted for its shell and its eggs

- ✋ Human activities and tourism are threatening beaches and coral reefs where sea turtles live

- ✋ Climate change is killing coral reefs that Hawksbill Sea Turtles feed on

- ✋ Often caught in fishing gear

30 **Go to page 42 to help me.**

A tropical night breeze brushes over the turtle. She will not wait to see her young hatch and scamper towards the ocean. Many will be grabbed by gulls and few will survive. The scientist counts as the last egg drops from this weary turtle mother. She writes '100' in her notes.

* n the warm waters of the Atlantic Ocean, Indian Ocean and Pacific Ocean *

* It is called a 'hawksbill' because of its narrow, sharp beak *

* It keeps coral reefs healthy by grazing and creating places for little fish to live *

31

Meet the
Staghorn Coral
Invertebrate
Acropora cervicornis

A pale story

Tipping over the edge of the dive-boat, the snorkeler tumbles into the tropical water. She is happy to see a ray swim by, but stares sadly at the spiky carpet of white coral all around her — it is nearly all dead.

Coral reefs are the 'rainforests of the sea' — full of colour and life. The orange, purple and pink Staghorn Corals help to create reefs in shallow waters, giving food and shelter to animals and seaweeds. But as climate change warms the ocean waters, the bright coral colours are fading and reefs are dying. The snorkeler searches for fish, but not many live here any more.

FACTS: * Staghorn Coral is found in the Caribbean Sea, in parts of the Gulf of Mexico, in the Australian Great Barrier Reef and in the waters of Southeast Asia*

* It is really important in creating reefs, which support a quarter of all marine life on Earth *

* Coral is an animal because it doesn't make its own food *

THE DANGER!

🖐 Listed as Critically Endangered on the IUCN Red List

🖐 Dying as the seas warm due to climate change

🖐 Killed by coral disease

🖐 Destroyed by storms and extreme weather also caused by climate change

🖐 Marine pollution

Go to page 42 to help me. 33

A small hairy story

Crawling amongst piles of wood on an Indian train, a bright blue spider is on the move. The train driver has no idea that a rare hairy spider is taking a ride. Arriving at the timber yard, the wood and this surprising little passenger are unloaded.

FACTS * The Peacock Tarantula lives in a small patch of forest in central southern India *

* It is very aggressive: its poisonous venom can cause humans a lot of pain *

* When it moults it lies on its back with its legs in the air, looking as if it is dead *

34

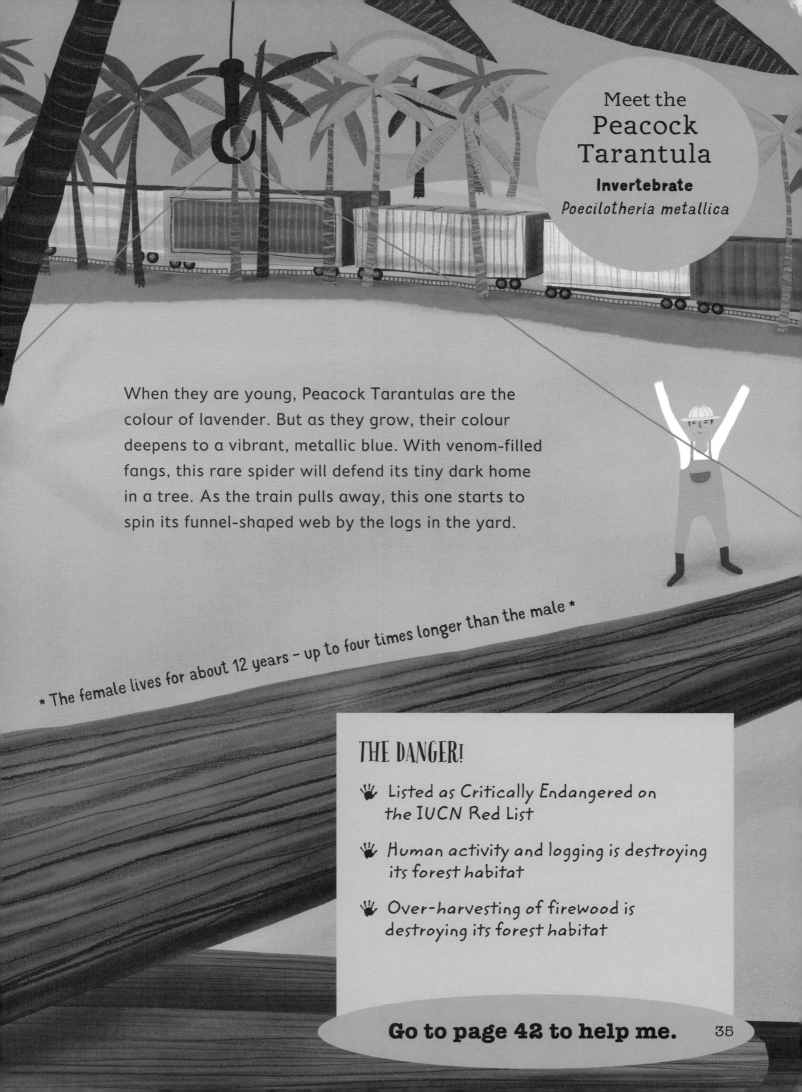

Meet the
Peacock Tarantula

Invertebrate
Poecilotheria metallica

When they are young, Peacock Tarantulas are the colour of lavender. But as they grow, their colour deepens to a vibrant, metallic blue. With venom-filled fangs, this rare spider will defend its tiny dark home in a tree. As the train pulls away, this one starts to spin its funnel-shaped web by the logs in the yard.

*The female lives for about 12 years – up to four times longer than the male *

THE DANGER!

- Listed as Critically Endangered on the IUCN Red List

- Human activity and logging is destroying its forest habitat

- Over-harvesting of firewood is destroying its forest habitat

Go to page 42 to help me.

Meet the
Largetooth Sawfish
Fish
Pristis pristis

A sharp story

This Largetooth Sawfish's bizarre snout is hopelessly tangled in a fishing net. It was looking for food on the muddy sea floor when it got stuck. But the fishermen in the boat above are unaware of the struggles of the huge shark-like ray far below.

Using its strange saw, this gigantic ray defends itself from sharks and other predators when it hunts at night. But its saw gets it into trouble. Twisted in netting, this one sinks towards the mud. The fishermen must cut it free when they find it in their net.

FACTS: ★ The Largetooth Sawfish lives in fresh and marine waters in tropical and sub-tropical ★ It kills fish by slashing its saw back and forth ★ It can live for 80 years ★

★ Newborn pups have fully formed saws, protected at birth in sheaths so they don't hurt their mothers ★

seas around the world, particularly around Australia ★

★ Its mouth is under its body and is full of tiny teeth ★

THE DANGER!

- 👋 Listed as Critically Endangered on the IUCN Red List

- 👋 Easily caught in fishing gear

- 👋 Hunted for its nose, meat, leather and fins for soup

- 👋 Caught for aquariums because of its bizarre shark-like shape

- 👋 Loss of habitat due to coastal development

Go to page 42 to help me.

Meet the
Bonobo
Mammal
Pan paniscus

A love story

A group of Bonobos are cuddling each other by the river, deep in the jungle. Treading carefully on the forest floor, a local park ranger creeps close enough to count these rare apes.

Like Chimpanzees, Bonobos are our very close relatives. But they are very different from Chimps, who are led by males and can be violent and aggressive. Bonobos are led by females and sort out problems with warmth and cuddles. They make close friends and spend time together happily in large groups. Watching baby Bonobos playing by the water's edge, the ranger is reminded of her own children playing at home.

FACTS ★ The Bonobo lives in forests near rivers only in The Democratic Republic of the Congo, Africa ★

★ Like Chimpanzees, the female Bonobo gives birth every five to six years ★

★ It was the last of the big apes to be discovered ★

★ It is mostly vegetarian, eating fruit and flowers ★

THE DANGER!

🖐 Listed as Endangered on the IUCN Red List

🖐 Poached for meat

🖐 Its forest habitat is cut down to grow crops

🖐 Wars and fighting surround the forests where it lives

Go to page 42 to help me.

Meet the
Giant Panda
Mammal

Ailuropoda melanoleuca

A good news story

Giant highways cut through the thick bamboo forests that are home to the Giant Panda. These bears are shy and finding a mate can be difficult, as their forests are divided by roads and cut down for farmland. But in remote places, workers are now digging tunnels so these rare animals can safely cross the road.

THE DANGER!

- 🖐 Downlisted from Endangered to Vulnerable on the IUCN Red List due to conservation efforts, but more action is still needed

- 🖐 Bamboo forests are being cut down for farmland

- 🖐 It may struggle to find a mate, as forests are isolated

- 🖐 About every 60 years the bamboo flowers and dies... with nothing to eat, pandas can starve

Go to page 42 to help me.

Giant Pandas only eat bamboo, so they are fussy about where they live. Too often they are isolated. By building panda tunnels so bears can find each other, the road workers are creating new hope for the survival of these lonely animals.

FACTS ★ The Giant Panda lives in thick bamboo forests, high in the mountains of Western China ★

★ A panda does everything slowly, because bamboo doesn't provide much energy ★

★ If she has two cubs, the Giant Panda will only look after one ★

Help us!

Find out how to help your favourite creature survive.

**Then turn back to page 8...
Pick Another Place.**

Peacock Tarantula

Help 'reforest' the Earth: plant a tree with your school to encourage wildlife: earthday.org

Do
Get stuck in!
Join a wildlife club or a charity helping endangered species.

Santa Catalina Rattlesnake

Track down the snake ID guide and learn to love your local snakes: arc-trust.org

Northern Rockhopper Penguin

Discover Project Pinnamin: rzss.org.uk or walk with penguins in 3D: birdlife.org

Ask
Inspire everyone to join in!
Talk to your parents, teachers and friends.

Panamanian Golden Frog

Play science games to save endangered species: arkive.org or discover the real frog hotel: marylandzoo.org

Save
Raise money!
Start a penny jar at school or hold a cake stall.

Staghorn Coral

Track down the *Coral Reef Education Pack* for your teacher: www.edgeofexistence.org

Red-headed Vulture

Play the Red List Amazing Species Quiz to get updates on the endangered animal that is most like you: support.iucnredlist.org/matching-game

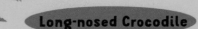

Blue Whale

Save whales from being tangled in fishing gear. Only buy sustainably caught fish:
fishandkids.msc.org

Long-nosed Crocodile

Share slide-show stories of this strange, watery creature:
gharialconservationalliance.org

Care

Want to help!
Fall in love
with a rare animal.

Largetooth Sawfish

Find out how to be a sawfish scientist: saveourseas.com

Giant Chinese Salamander

Find out how to help endangered species by becoming a *Wildlife Champion*:
edgeofexistence.org/champions

Learn

Do some digging!
Read a book, go online,
talk to an expert.

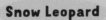

Giant Panda

Join an organisation that celebrates and saves giant pandas: wwf.panda.org

Snow Leopard

Share the secrets of snow leopards by sending ecards:
snowleopard.org

Hawksbill Sea Turtle

Find and follow the *Turtle Code* on tropical holidays: mcsuk.org

Share

Spread the word!
Make a poster or write a poem
to read out loud.

Sunda Pangolin

Find the colouring sheet that will bring these little-known creatures to life: savepangolins.org

Bonobo

Find and share folk stories and songs about your relatives:
bonobo.org

Please note that all urls are accurate at the time of going to press.

The story of the IUCN Red List

✋ In 1933 an American conservationist, John C. Phillips, was worried about the number of different rare animals, plants and fungi threatened with extinction, so he began to make a list.

✋ The list was adopted in 1949 by a big new international organisation called the IUCN (International Union for Conservation of Nature) and made publicly available in 1964; it has grown into The IUCN Red List of Threatened Species™ which describes the global status of animals, plants and fungi.

✋ An online campaign, *Amazing Species*, raises awareness of the IUCN Red List, which currently lists over 88,000 species.

✋ The IUCN Red List is updated at least once every year and aims to collect data on 160,000 species by 2020.

✋ In 2008 humans were listed in the category of 'Least Concern'.

✋ The goal of the IUCN Red List is 'to provide information and analyses on the status, trends and threats to species to inform and catalyse action for biodiversity conservation'.

To find out more go to: iucnredlist.org

There are all sorts of creatures on the IUCN Red List...

Please note that the IUCN Red List status of the 15 creatures in this book is accurate at the time of going to press.

Turn the page to match names to the 15 creatures in this book, plus discover 60 more!

1. Burmese Roofed Turtle
2. Aye Aye
3. Pygmy Raccoon
4. Olm
5. Puma
6. Porbeagle
7. Orangutan
8. Hector's Dolphin
9. Southern Three-banded Armadillo
10. Green Humphead Parrot Fish
11. Western Lowland Gorilla
12. Galapagos Sealion
13. Brown Spider Monkey
14. Polar Bear
15. Sir David's Long-beaked Echidna
16. Whale Shark
17. Far Eastern Curlew
18. Golden-rumped Sengi
19. Bombus Dahlbomii
20. Sperm Whale

21. Desert Rain Frog
22. Sumatran Rhinoceros
23. Sumatran Tiger
24. Pygmy Hippopotamus
25. Jerdon's Courser
26. Pink River Dolphin
27. Tarzan's Chameleon
28. Marvellous Spatuletail Hummingbird
29. Darwin's Frog
30. Rapa Fruit-dove
31. Steppe Eagle
32. Okapi
33. Volcano Rabbit
34. Lord Howe Island Stick Insect
35. Angel Shark
36. Malay Tapir
37. Proboscis Monkey
38. Kakapo
39. Giant Devil Ray
40. Red Wolf

41. Northern Brown Kiwi
42. Addax
43. Northern Quoll
44. Cuban Greater Funnel-eared Bat
45. Asian Elephant
46. Ring-tailed Lemur
47. Banded Cotinga
48. American Burying Beetle
49. Lion-tailed Macaque
50. Hyacinth Macaw
51. Sun Bear
52. Black Rhinoceros
53. Yellow-eared Parrot
54. Pygmy Three-toed Sloth
55. Devil's Hole Pupfish
56. Grey-breasted Parakeet
57. Przewalski's Horse
58. Red Panda
59. Hammerhead Shark
60. Bahia Tapaculo

About the Author and Illustrator

Catherine Barr campaigned to protect endangered species with Greenpeace for many years. She then became an editor at the Natural History Museum before moving to the Welsh borders and becoming a children's author. She lives in Herefordshire with her partner and two girls, for whom she wrote her first book, *The Story of Life*, now an internationally successful series. Catherine writes a wide variety of information books to spark curiosity and inspire action to protect the natural world.

• • •

Anne Wilson was born on Ascension Island in the South Atlantic, but now lives in Reading, England. She has an MA in Illustration from Central Saint Martins, London. Her artistic process balances the traditional and digital. A scalpel, dip pen and inks sit side by side with her Wacom tablet, Mac and Photoshop. She loves the physical processes of colour mixing and mark making. The results are scanned and imported into Photoshop to create a final image.